Junior Great Books®

Reader's Journal

Series 3   Book One

This book belongs to:

_____

The Great Books Foundation
A nonprofit educational organization

The interpretive discussion program that moves
students toward excellence in reading comprehension,
critical thinking, and writing

9 8
Printed in the United States of America

Cover art by Vivienne Flesher. Copyright © 2006 by Vivienne Flesher.
Text and cover design by William Seabright, William Seabright & Associates.
Interior design by Think Design Group.

Published and distributed by

The Great Books Foundation
A nonprofit educational organization
35 East Wacker Drive, Suite 400
Chicago, IL 60601

Welcome to Your Reader's Journal

This Reader's Journal is a place for you to collect your thoughts about the Junior Great Books stories you read and discuss in class. Here, you can also be an artist and a poet, while discovering some secrets to becoming a strong reader and writer.

There are many parts of the Reader's Journal to explore:

Writing Notebook allows you to gather some of your favorite pieces of writing in one place after you polish them up.

Curious Words is where you can record all the strange, fun words you come across while reading. You don't have to memorize these words—you get to play with them, rolling them around on your tongue or using them to make up messages and rhymes.

The **glossary** contains unusual or difficult words from the stories you've read. Look here for definitions that will help you better understand what you're reading.

Are you hunting for a **keeper question**, or do you have your **Head in the Clouds**? Maybe you're **Building Your Answer**, **Writing to Explain** or **Explore**, or getting **Into Reading**. Whatever you're up to, this Reader's Journal belongs to you. It's the place for your great ideas.

Contents

The Banza

Haitian folktale as told by Diane Wolkstein

Into Reading

Asking Questions

Asking questions is an important part of understanding what you're reading. Read the following two passages from the story and write a question that you have about each one. Remember your questions as you read the story a second time.

Passage 1 (page 16)

"A musician!" said the chief, laughing. "So you wish to play us a song?"
"No!" said Cabree.
"No?" echoed the leader. And all the tigers took a step closer to Cabree.
Teegra! Cabree wanted to shout. But Teegra was far away, and she was alone, surrounded by the tigers. No, she was not completely alone. She still had the banza Teegra had given her.

Your question after reading this passage:

_____

_____

_____

_____

_____

Passage 2 (page 20)

Cabree looked at the trembling tiger. All she had done was to play the banza and sing what was in her heart. So Teegra's auntie was right. Her heart had protected her. Her heart and her banza.

"Please!" begged the leader. "I'll do whatever you wish."

"Then go at once to Teegra, the little tiger who lives near the cave. Tell Teegra: 'Today Cabree's heart and the banza are one.' "

Your question after reading this passage:

_____

_____

_____

_____

Use your imagination! Choose one of the topics in the clouds
and draw a picture or write a little more about the story.
(If you have time, you can choose more than one topic.)

My favorite part
of the story

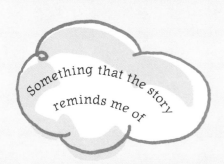

Something that the story
reminds me of

Something from the
story that I'm still
curious about

in the Clouds

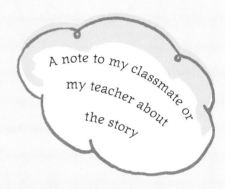

A note to my classmate or my teacher about the story

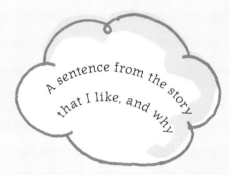

A sentence from the story that I like, and why

Why I like/do not like this story

Building Your Answer

The focus question:

_____

_____

_____

_____

Your answer before the discussion:

_____

_____

_____

_____

Your answer after the discussion (you may change or add to your first answer):

_____

_____

_____

_____

_____

Writing to Explain

A Clear Idea

When you answer a question, your words should help your readers understand what you're answering. For example, think about this question and answer:

- **Question:** Why is Cabree able to stand up to the tigers?

- **Complete answer:** *Cabree can stand up to the tigers* because she feels good hearing the music.

As you write your answer to the focus question, think about how to make your sentence say exactly what you mean.

Read the answers you wrote on the facing Building Your Answer page. In the space below, rewrite your answer into a complete statement.

Your complete answer to the focus question:

_____

_____

_____

_____

Writing to Explore
A Friendly Letter

Write a friendly letter from one character in "The Banza" to another. Choose which character will write the letter and which character will receive the letter. You may use your class notes from the board and your own ideas as you write.

A Letter from _____

Dear _____,

_____

_____

_____

_____

_____

_____

_____

Your friend,

_____

The Man Whose Trade Was Tricks

Georgian folktale as told by George and Helen Papashvily

Keeper Question

In the space below, write a **keeper question** about the story that came into your mind during the first reading, while sharing questions, or even right now. Choose one that no one has completely answered yet, and keep it in your mind during the second reading. If you still have the question after reading, continue to think about it—you picked a real keeper!

Your keeper question:

_____

_____

_____

_____

Asking questions is an important part of understanding what you're reading. Read the following three passages from the story and write a question that you have about each one. Remember your questions as you read the story a second time.

Passage 1 (page 24)

Each year [the king] took such a heavy rent that no matter how hard the villagers worked when harvest time came, nothing was left for them but the middlings of their own wheat and a few crooked tree stumps.

Your question after reading this passage:

what is a midling?

Passage 2 (page 26)

"Sit down," the king said. "So you think you are the trickiest man in my kingdom?"

"Tricking is my trade," Shahkro answered.

"Try to trick me then," the king commanded. "But I warn you," he added, "it cannot be done for I am so tricky myself."

"I can see that," Shahkro said. "I wish I had known all this before. I would have come prepared."

Your question after reading this passage:

The king doesent know if he is triky he only thinks he is so why spuld he take such a chance?

Passage 3 (page 32)

"Wait," [Shahkro] said, "I will take another reward. Because on second thought you do use your head. It keeps your hat from lying on your shoulders. Give me instead your forest and all the fields around it for my village people to use for their own."

Your question after reading this passage:

why didnt he becoume king so he could give more to his peadpole?

Use your imagination! Choose one of the topics in the clouds and draw a picture or write a little more about the story. (If you have time, you can choose more than one topic.)

My favorite part of the story

Something that the story reminds me of

Something from the story that I'm still curious about

in the Clouds

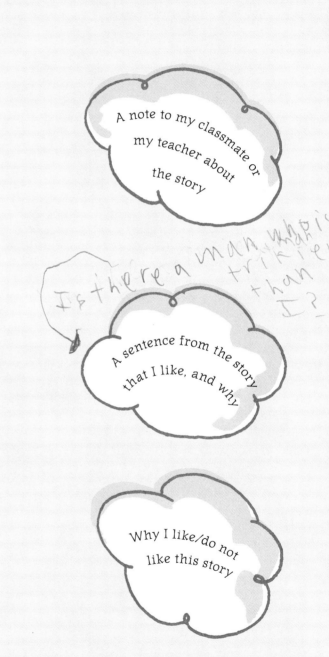

A note to my classmate or my teacher about the story

Is there a man who is trickier than I?

A sentence from the story that I like, and why

Why I like/do not like this story

Building Your Answer

The focus question:

_____

_____

_____

_____

Your answer before the discussion:

_____

_____

_____

_____

Your answer after the discussion *(you may change or add to your first answer)*:

_____

_____

_____

_____

_____

_____

Writing to Explain
Introducing Your Evidence

Prewriting Notes

Write your complete sentence answering the focus question in the large circle. Then, in the other circles, write details from the story that support your idea.

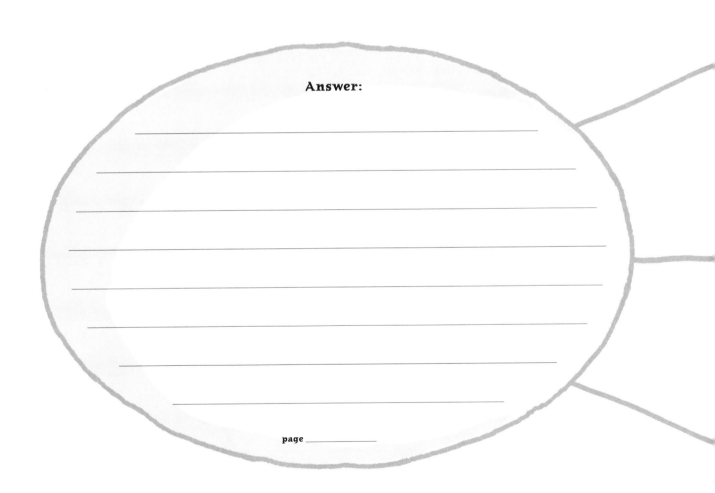

Answer:

_____

_____

_____

_____

_____

_____

page _____

Writing to Explain
Introducing Your Evidence

Evidence:

_____

_____

_____

_____

page _____

Evidence:

_____

_____

_____

_____

page _____

Evidence:

_____

_____

_____

_____

page _____

Prewriting Notes

Think of some reputations you would like to have, then think of things you could do to get these reputations. Fill in the chart below. Make sure that each thing you could do to earn that reputation is stated in a complete sentence. For example, instead of writing "Study hard" as a way to get a reputation for being a good student, write: "I will study for one hour the night before every test."

Reputation	What I Will Do to Get It
_____	_____
_____	_____
_____	_____
_____	_____

Reputation	What I Will Do to Get It
_____	_____
_____	_____
_____	_____
_____	_____

The Fisherman and His Wife

Brothers Grimm

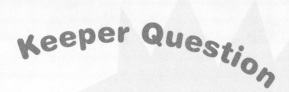

Keeper Question

In the space below, write a keeper question about the story that came into your mind during the first reading, while sharing questions, or even right now. Choose one that no one has completely answered yet, and keep it in your mind during the second reading. If you still have the question after reading, continue to think about it—you picked a real keeper!

Your keeper question:

_____

_____

_____

_____

Asking questions is an important part of understanding what you're reading. Read the following three passages from the story and write a question that you have about each one. Remember your questions when you read the story a second time.

Passage 1 (pages 35–36)

Oh, man of the sea, come listen to me,
For Alice, my wife, the plague of my life,
Has sent me to ask a boon of thee.

Then the fish came swimming up and said, "Now then, what does she want?"

"Oh," said the man, "my wife says that I should have asked you for something when I caught you. She does not want to live any longer in the hut and would rather have a cottage."

"Go home," said the fish. "She has it already."

Your question after reading this passage: _____

_____

_____

_____

Passage 2 (page 37)

All went well for a week or fortnight. Then the wife said, "Look here, husband, the cottage is really too small. I think the fish had better give us a larger house. I should like very much to live in a large stone castle. So go to your fish, and he will send us a castle."

"Oh, my dear wife!" said the man. "The cottage is good enough. What do we want a castle for?"

"Go along," said the wife. "He might just as well give it to us as not. Do as I say."

The man did not want to go, and he said to himself, "It is not the right thing to do."

Your question after reading this passage: _____

_____

_____

_____

Passage 3 (page 47)

Oh, man of the sea, come listen to me,
For Alice, my wife, the plague of my life,
Has sent me to ask a boon of thee.

"Well, what now?" said the fish.
"Oh, dear!" said the man. "She wants to order about the sun and moon."
"Go home with you," said the fish, "and you will find her in the old hut."

Your question after reading this passage: _____

_____

_____

_____

Use your imagination! Choose one of the topics in the clouds
and draw a picture or write a little more about the story.
(If you have time, you can choose more than one topic.)

My favorite part
of the story

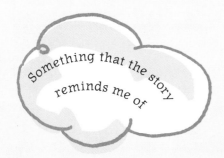

Something that the story
reminds me of

Something from the
story that I'm still
curious about

in the Clouds

A time I got what I wished for

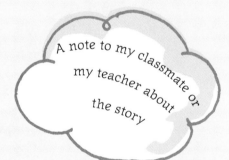

A note to my classmate or my teacher about the story

Why I like/do not like this story

Building Your Answer

The focus question:

_____

_____

_____

_____

Your answer before the discussion:

_____

_____

_____

_____

Your answer after the discussion *(you may change or add to your first answer):*

_____

_____

_____

_____

_____

_____

_____

Writing to Explain
Responding to a Classmate

Have your partner tell you how he or she answered the four questions. Now write a short letter to your partner about the idea he or she explained to you.

Dear _____,

The part I liked best in your answer was _____

_____

_____

_____

_____

I would like to know more about _____

_____

_____

_____

_____

Sincerely,

_____

Writing to Explore
A Wish List

Prewriting Notes

The fish will give you five wishes. Decide what you will wish for, and write each wish in the place that best describes the kind of wish you are making.

To Do

_____

_____

_____

To Have

_____

_____

_____

_____

To Be

_____

_____

_____

Writing to Explore
A Wish List

Writing a Draft

Now write your wishes in complete sentences. For example, instead of "To go to an amusement park," write: "I wish I could go to an amusement park with my best friend, Jackie."

1. _____

_____

_____

2. _____

_____

_____

3. _____

_____

_____

4. _____

_____

_____

Ooka and the Honest Thief

Japanese folktale as told by I. G. Edmonds

Keeper Question

In the space below, write a keeper question about the story that came into your mind during the first reading, while sharing questions, or even right now. Choose one that no one has completely answered yet, and keep it in your mind during the second reading. If you still have the question after reading, continue to think about it—you picked a real keeper!

Your keeper question:

_____

_____

_____

_____

Into Reading

Making Connections

Connecting your knowledge and personal experience to a story helps you make better sense of the story.

Look in the story for places where you marked a **C**. Below, use your own words to describe what happened in the story. Then write how that part of the story **connects** to something in your own life.

Something that happens in the story:

_____

_____

_____

_____

_____ **page** _____

Your personal connection to what happens in the story:

_____

_____

_____

_____

_____

Use your imagination! Choose one of the topics in the clouds
and draw a picture or write a little more about the story.
(If you have time, you can choose more than one topic.)

My favorite part
of the story

Something that the story
reminds me of

A picture of a character
in the story

Something that my keeper
question makes me
think of

in the Clouds

A note to Ooka

A sentence from the story that I like, and why

Why I like/do not like this story

A part of the story that I'm still wondering about

Building Your Answer

The focus question:

_____

_____

_____

_____

Your answer before the discussion:

_____

_____

_____

_____

Your answer after the discussion (you may change or add to your first answer):

_____

_____

_____

_____

_____

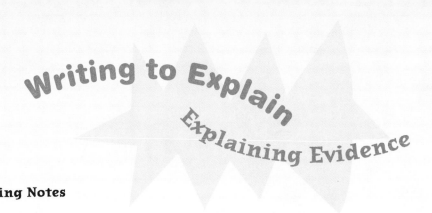

Writing to Explain
Explaining Evidence

Prewriting Notes

In the left-hand column below, write some evidence that shows Ooka being fair or unfair. On the right-hand side, explain **why** you think the evidence shows that Ooka is being fair or unfair.

Evidence	**Explanation**

Ooka is fair or unfair (circle one) **when he:**

_____

_____

_____

_____ **page** _____

This shows Ooka being fair or unfair (circle one) **because:**

_____

_____

_____

_____ **page** _____

Ooka is fair or unfair (circle one) **when he:**

_____

_____

_____

_____ **page** _____

This shows Ooka being fair or unfair (circle one) **because:**

_____

_____

_____

_____ **page** _____

Writing to Explain
Explaining Evidence

Evidence	Explanation

Ooka is fair **or** unfair (circle one) **when he:**

_____

_____

_____

_____ **page** _____

This shows Ooka being fair **or** unfair (circle one) **because:**

_____

_____

_____

_____ **page** _____

Ooka is fair **or** unfair (circle one) **when he:**

_____

_____

_____

_____ **page** _____

This shows Ooka being fair **or** unfair (circle one) **because:**

_____

_____

_____

_____ **page** _____

Writing to Explore
Gonta's Diary

Prewriting Notes

Pretend you are Gonta and write some ideas about Gonta's first week at his new job. Then, on the right side, write how you might feel if those events happened.

What happened:

My feelings:

MONDAY I start my new job today.

I feel excited, but also very nervous!

TUESDAY

WEDNESDAY

THURSDAY

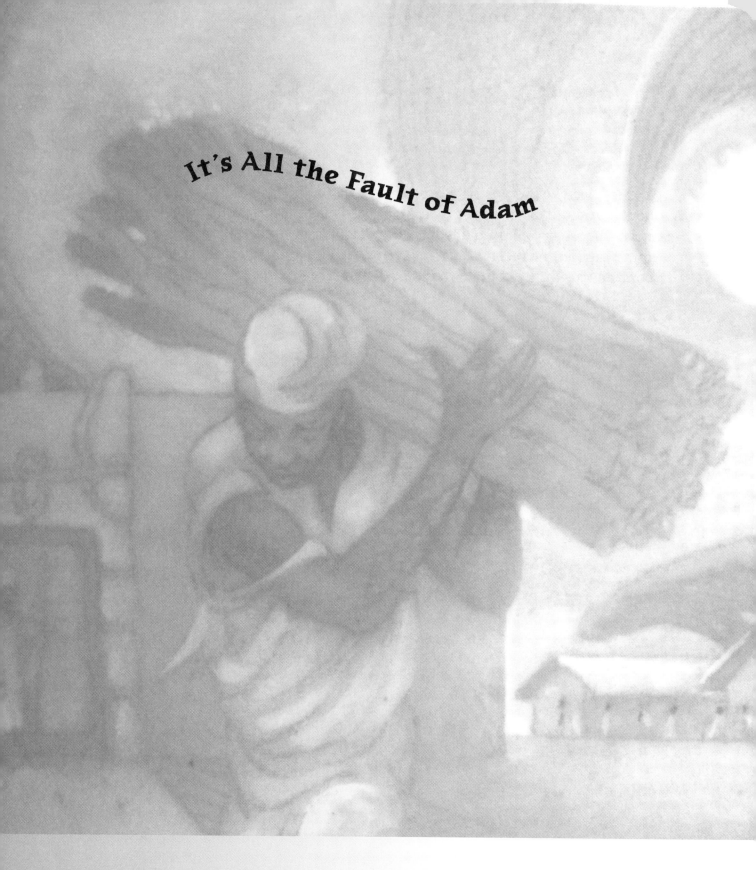

It's All the Fault of Adam

Nigerian folktale as told by Barbara Walker

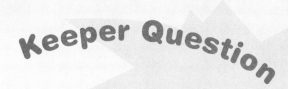

Keeper Question

In the space below, write a keeper question about the story that came into your mind during the first reading, while sharing questions, or even right now. Choose one that no one has completely answered yet, and keep it in your mind during the second reading. If you still have the question after reading, continue to think about it—you picked a real keeper!

Your keeper question:

_____

_____

_____

_____

Into Reading

Making Connections

Connecting your knowledge and personal experience to a story helps you make better sense of the story.

Look in the story for places where you marked a **C**. Below, use your own words to describe what happened in the story. Then write how that part of the story **connects** to something in your own life.

Something that happens in the story:

_____

_____

_____

_____

_____

_____

_____ **page** _____

Your personal connection to what happens in the story:

_____

_____

_____

_____

_____

_____

_____

Use your imagination! Choose one of the topics in the clouds
and draw a picture or write a little more about the story.
(If you have time, you can choose more than one topic.)

My favorite part of the story

Something that the story reminds me of

A part of the story that I thought was funny

A picture of the king

in the Clouds

A note to Iyapò

A sentence from the story that I like, and why

Why I like/do not like this story

A part of the story that I'm still wondering about

Building Your Answer

The focus question:

_____

_____

_____

Your answer before the discussion:

_____

_____

_____

Your answer after the discussion (you may change or add to your first answer):

_____

_____

_____

Evidence that supports your answer:

1. _____

_____

2. _____

_____

Writing to Explain
Say It in Your Own Words

Choose a short passage from the story that you like. Write it below.

A passage from page _____ :

_____

_____

_____

_____

_____

Now **paraphrase** the passage—retell the passage in your own words—below.

_____

_____

_____

_____

_____

Writing to Explore
It's All the Fault of...

Prewriting Notes

Write about something that annoys or frustrates you—your gripe—in the space below.

Your gripe:

_____

_____

_____

_____

Whom or what are you going to blame for your gripe?

It's all the fault of _____ **!**

Now write some of the reasons you are blaming this person or thing for your gripe.

1. _____

_____

2. _____

_____

3. _____

_____

Writing to Explore
It's All the Fault of...

Writing a Draft

Use your prewriting notes to write about your gripe in the space below. Remember to write in complete, detailed sentences.

It's All the Fault of _____ **!**

My big gripe today is:

_____

_____

_____

_____

It's all the fault of _____ **because:**

_____

_____

_____

_____

The Monster Who Grew Small

Joan Grant

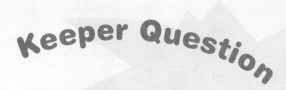

Keeper Question

In the space below, write a keeper question about the story that came into your mind during the first reading, while sharing questions, or even right now. Choose one that no one has completely answered yet, and keep it in your mind during the second reading. If you still have the question after reading, continue to think about it—you picked a real keeper!

Your keeper question:

_____

_____

_____

_____

Into Reading

Making Connections

Connecting your knowledge and personal experience to a story helps you make better sense of the story.

Look in the story for places where you marked a **C**. Below, use your own words to describe what happened in the story. Then write how that part of the story **connects** to something in your own life.

Something that happens in the story:

_____

_____

_____

_____

_____

_____ **page** _____

Your personal connection to what happens in the story:

_____

_____

_____

_____

_____

_____

Use your imagination! Choose one of the topics in the clouds and draw a picture or write a little more about the story.
(If you have time, you can choose more than one topic.)

My favorite part of the story

Something that the story reminds me of

Something from the story that scared me

A picture of the hare talking to Miobi

in the Clouds

A note to Miobi

A sentence from the story that I like, and why

Why I like/do not like this story

A part of the story that I'm still wondering about

Building Your Answer

The focus question:

_____

_____

_____

Your answer before the discussion:

_____

_____

_____

Your answer after the discussion (you may change or add to your first answer)**:**

_____

_____

_____

An answer you heard in discussion that is different from yours:

_____

_____

_____

Writing to Explain
Responding to a Classmate

Prewriting Notes

Listen carefully to your partner explain his or her answer to the focus question.

Your partner's answer: _____

_____

_____

_____ Partner's name: _____

Explain in your own words the reasons your partner gave for this answer.

_____

_____

_____

Now think about whether you agree or disagree with your partner's answer. Circle one:

Agree / Disagree

Why do you agree / disagree ? _____

_____

_____

Writing to Explore
A Letter of Advice

Prewriting Notes

With your partner, pretend that you have a problem that you both would like to ask Miobi about. Then answer each question below.

The problem: _____

_____

_____

Why do you think Miobi can help you with this problem? _____

_____

_____

When and where do you have this problem? _____

_____

_____

_____

Why does this problem happen? (Guess if you're not sure.) _____

_____

_____

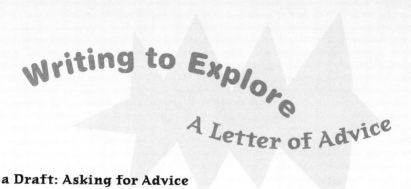

Writing a Draft: Asking for Advice

On your own, write your letter to Miobi asking him for advice, using the answers you and your partner came up with to help you write.

Dear Miobi,

I am writing to you because _____

_____

_____

_____

_____

_____

_____

_____

_____

_____

_____

Sincerely,

_____

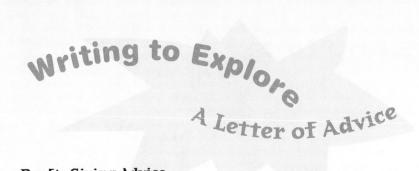

Writing a Draft: Giving Advice

Now you and your partner can trade journals with another pair of classmates. Read the letter in your classmate's Reader's Journal on page 61. Talk with your partner about what advice Miobi might give to solve this problem. Then write a letter on your own in the space below as if you are Miobi trying to solve the problem.

Dear _____,

_____

_____

_____

_____

_____

_____

_____

I hope this will solve your problem.

Sincerely,

Miobi

The Selkie Girl

Scottish folktale as told by Susan Cooper

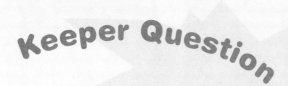

Keeper Question

In the space below, write a keeper question about the story that came into your mind during the first reading, while sharing questions, or even right now. Choose one that no one has completely answered yet, and keep it in your mind during the second reading. If you still have the question after reading, continue to think about it—you picked a real keeper!

Your keeper question:

_____

_____

_____

_____

Visualizing helps you create pictures in your mind as you read a story. These pictures could come from any of your five senses (seeing, hearing, touching, tasting, or smelling). It's like seeing a movie or a play in your mind.

Look in the story for places that you marked with a **V**. Write down a passage you marked below. Then describe what you **visualize** using any of your senses.

A passage that you marked with a V:

_____

_____

_____

_____

_____

_____ **page** _____

What you visualize:

_____

_____

_____

_____

_____

_____

Use your imagination! Choose one of the topics in the clouds and draw a picture or write a little more about the story. (If you have time, you can choose more than one topic.)

My favorite scene in the story

Something that the story reminds me of

Something from the story that I'm still wondering about

A place in the story that I'd like to visit

in the Clouds

A note to my best friend about the story

A sentence from the story that I like, and why

Why I like/do not like this story

What I think might happen after the story ends

Building Your Answer

The focus question:

_____

_____

_____

_____

Your answer before the discussion:

_____

_____

_____

_____

Your answer after the discussion (you may change or add to your first answer):

_____

_____

_____

_____

_____

Writing to Explain
A Beginning Essay

Prewriting Notes

Look at your answer after the discussion on page 68. Then write some evidence from the story that supports your answer.

Evidence that supports your answer:

1. _____

   _____

2. _____

   _____

3. _____

   _____

A strong opening sentence for your essay:

_____

_____

_____

Writing to Explain
A Beginning Essay

Writing a Draft

Write a short essay that includes your answer to the focus question and gives evidence to support your answer. Start your essay with the opening sentence you wrote.

_____

_____

_____

_____

_____

_____

_____

_____

_____

_____

_____

_____

_____

_____

_____

_____

Writing to Explain
A Beginning Essay

Use this page if you need more room.

_____

_____

_____

_____

_____

_____

_____

_____

_____

_____

_____

_____

_____

_____

_____

_____

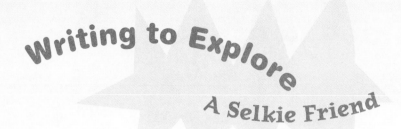

Writing to Explore
A Selkie Friend

Prewriting Notes

Imagine that you have a selkie friend of your own. List some details to describe your friend. Your details might include what your friend looks or sounds like, what he or she likes or dislikes, or what his or her personality is like. Then circle the most interesting detail to begin your draft on the next page.

1. _____

_____

2. _____

_____

3. _____

_____

4. _____

_____

5. _____

_____

Writing to Explore
A Selkie Friend

Writing a Draft

Now write about your selkie friend using complete, detailed sentences. Use your most interesting detail first so your readers will want to read more.

Writing to Explore
A Selkie Friend

Use this page if you need more room.

_____

_____

_____

_____

_____

_____

_____

_____

_____

_____

_____

_____

_____

_____

_____

_____

_____

_____

The Mushroom Man

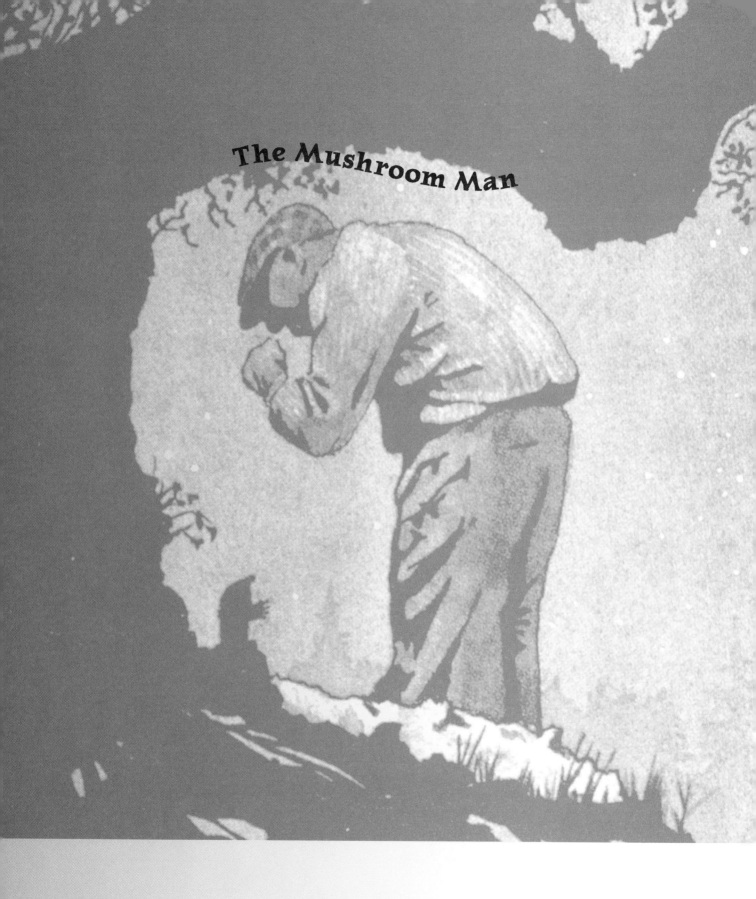

Ethel Pochocki

In the space below, write a keeper question about the story that came into your mind during the first reading, while sharing questions, or even right now. Choose one that no one has completely answered yet, and keep it in your mind during the second reading. If you still have the question after reading, continue to think about it—you picked a real keeper!

Your keeper question:

_____

_____

_____

_____

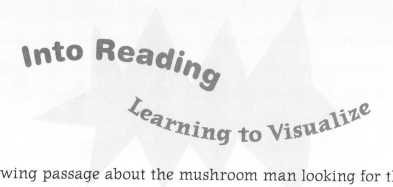

Into Reading
Learning to Visualize

Read the following passage about the mushroom man looking for the cat. Describe what you visualize, and write about how you think he is feeling.

Passage (page 103)

The mushroom man searched, calling out to her, pleading for her return, but Beatrice never came back. He sat on the bench, sighing sadly. Perhaps it was his fate to be alone.

What you visualize when you read this passage: _____

_____

_____

_____

How you think the mushroom man feels in this passage: _____

_____

_____

_____

Think about a memory from your own life that helps you understand how the mushroom man feels, and write it below.

I know how the mushroom man feels because: _____

_____

_____

_____

Use your imagination! Choose one of the topics in the clouds
and draw a picture or write a little more about the story.
(If you have time, you can choose more than one topic.)

My favorite part of the story

Something that the story reminds me of

A picture of the mole

Something that my keeper question makes me think of

in the Clouds

A note to the mushroom man

A sentence from the story that I like, and why

Why I like/do not like this story

An animal I would be friends with, and why

Building Your Answer

The focus question:

_____

_____

_____

Your answer before the discussion:

_____

_____

_____

Your answer after the discussion _(you may change or add to your first answer):_

_____

_____

_____

A quote or brief passage from the story that supports your answer:

_____

_____

_____

_____

Writing to Explain
Explaining Your Answer

Prewriting Notes

Look at your answer after the discussion on page 80. Below, write some evidence that supports your answer. Then explain how you think it supports your answer.

Evidence: _____

_____

_____

_____

_____

How your evidence supports your answer: _____

_____

_____

_____

_____

_____

Explain your answer and evidence to a partner. If your partner does not understand something, decide together what you can add or what words you can use to make it clearer.

Writing to Explain
Explaining Your Answer

Writing a Draft

On your own, write an essay that tells your answer to the focus question and explains why each piece of evidence supports your answer.

_____

_____

_____

_____

_____

_____

_____

_____

_____

_____

_____

_____

_____

_____

_____

_____

Writing to Explain
Explaining Your Answer

Use this page if you need more room.

_____

_____

_____

_____

_____

_____

_____

_____

_____

_____

_____

_____

_____

_____

_____

_____

_____

_____

Writing to Explore
The Perfect Animal Friend

Prewriting Notes

In the chart below, write some details about a person you know and an animal you think would be a perfect friend for this person. Remember that your person and the animal should be the same in some ways, just like the mushroom man and the mole.

Details	Person:	Animal:
Looks like		
Sounds like		
Likes to do		
Likes to eat		
Favorite place to be		

Writing to Explore
The Perfect Animal Friend

Writing a Draft

Write your description of the person you know and that person's animal friend. Remember to explain why you think the person and the animal would be a perfect match.

The Perfect Animal Friend for _____

_____

_____

_____

_____

_____

_____

_____

_____

_____

_____

_____

_____

_____

_____

_____

Writing to Explore
The Perfect Animal Friend

Use this page if you need more room.

_____

_____

_____

_____

_____

_____

_____

_____

_____

_____

_____

_____

_____

_____

_____

The Princess and the Beggar

Korean folktale as told by Anne Sibley O'Brien

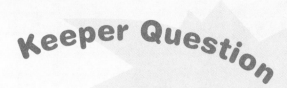

Keeper Question

In the space below, write a keeper question about the story that came into your mind during the first reading, while sharing questions, or even right now. Choose one that no one has completely answered yet, and keep it in your mind during the second reading. If you still have the question after reading, continue to think about it—you picked a real keeper!

Your keeper question:

_____

_____

_____

_____

Into Reading
Learning to Visualize

You may visualize something from the story the first time you read it, but when you read it a second or third time, you might add to or change your mental image.

In the space below, write the page and paragraph numbers of a passage you marked with a **V**. Describe what you **visualize** when you read it.

Your passage: page _____, paragraph _____

What you visualize while reading this passage:

_____

_____

_____

_____

_____

Now read the passage a second time. Add more details to your original description, or write about how your visualization changed.

How your visualization changed:

_____

_____

_____

_____

_____

Use your imagination! Choose one of the topics in the clouds
and draw a picture or write a little more about the story.
(If you have time, you can choose more than one topic.)

My favorite part of the story

Something that the story reminds me of

Something from the story that I'm still wondering about

Something that my keeper question makes me think of

in the Clouds

A note to Pabo Ondal

A sentence from the story that I like, and why

Why I like/do not like this story

The character that I'm most like, and why

Building Your Answer

The focus question:

_____

_____

_____

Your answer before the discussion:

_____

_____

_____

Your answer after the discussion (you may change or add to your first answer):

_____

_____

_____

An answer you heard in discussion that is different from yours:

_____

_____

_____

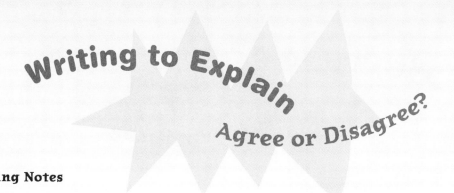

Writing to Explain
Agree or Disagree?

Prewriting Notes

Look at your answer from after the discussion on page 92. Write evidence and how it supports your answer below. Then share it with a partner.

Your partner's name: _____

Evidence:	**How it supports your answer:**

1. _____   1. _____

   _____   _____

   _____   _____

2. _____   2. _____

   _____   _____

   _____   _____

What your partner and you agree about: _____

_____

_____

What you do not agree about: _____

_____

_____

Writing a Draft

Write a paragraph with your partner that explains how you agree and disagree about the story.

_____

_____

_____

_____

_____

_____

_____

_____

_____

_____

_____

_____

_____

_____

_____

_____

Writing to Explain
Agree or Disagree?

Use this page if you need more room.

_____

_____

_____

_____

_____

_____

_____

_____

_____

_____

_____

_____

_____

_____

_____

_____

_____

_____

_____

_____

Writing to Explore

A Poem About Somebody Special

Prewriting Notes

In the left-hand column below, write a description of a person who is special to you. Then, in the right-hand column, write a description of a flower, a plant, or a tree that reminds you of the person you described.

Somebody special: _____

A flower or a plant: _____

_____

_____

_____

_____

_____

_____

_____

_____

_____

_____

_____

_____

_____

_____

_____

_____

_____

_____

_____

_____

_____

_____

_____

Writing a Draft

Now write a poem comparing the person to the flower or the plant that you chose, using your prewriting notes to help you.

A Poem About _____

_____

_____

_____

_____

_____

_____

_____

_____

_____

_____

_____

_____

_____

_____

_____

The Fire on the Mountain

Ethiopian Folktale as told by Harold Courlander and Wolf Leslau

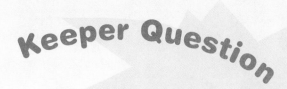

Keeper Question

In the space below, write a keeper question about the story that came into your mind during the first reading, while sharing questions, or even right now. Choose one that no one has completely answered yet, and keep it in your mind during the second reading. If you still have the question after reading, continue to think about it—you picked a real keeper!

Your keeper question:

_____

_____

_____

_____

Into Reading
Putting It All Together

You practiced asking **questions**, making **connections**, and **visualizing** during your first reading. Look at your notes and choose one passage you marked with a **?**, one with a **C**, and one with a **V**. Below, explain how you used each strategy.

The passage you marked with a **?** is on **page** _____, **paragraph** _____.

Your question about this passage: _____

_____

_____

The passage you marked with a **C** is on **page** _____, **paragraph** _____.

Your connection to this passage: _____

_____

_____

The passage you marked with a **V** is on **page** _____, **paragraph** _____.

Your visualization about this passage: _____

_____

_____

Use your imagination! Choose one of the topics in the clouds and draw a picture or write a little more about the story. (If you have time, you can choose more than one topic.)

My favorite part of the story

Something that the story reminds me of

A picture of the dinner party

A fire on the mountaintop

in the Clouds

A note to Arha on the mountain

A sentence from the story that I like, and why

Why I like/do not like this story

Something in the story that I'm still wondering about

Building Your Answer

The focus question:

_____

_____

_____

_____

Your answer before the discussion:

_____

_____

_____

_____

Your answer after the discussion (you may change or add to your first answer):

_____

_____

_____

Evidence from the Story / Something from discussion **that supports your answer** (circle one):

_____

_____

_____

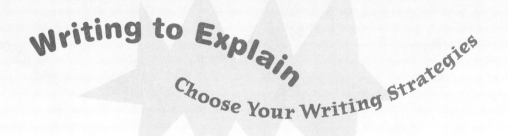

Writing to Explain
Choose Your Writing Strategies

Prewriting Notes

Look at your answer on the Building Your Answer page on page 104.
Then make a **list / web / chart** (circle one) that shows:

• Evidence from the story that supports your answer, told in your own words

• How your evidence supports your answer

• The order in which your evidence will appear in your essay

Writing a Draft

Write your essay, using your prewriting notes, in the space below.

_____

_____

_____

_____

_____

_____

_____

_____

_____

_____

_____

_____

_____

_____

_____

_____

_____

_____

_____

_____

Writing to Explain

Choose Your Writing Strategies

Use this page if you need more room.

_____

_____

_____

_____

_____

_____

_____

_____

_____

_____

_____

_____

_____

_____

_____

_____

_____

_____

_____

Writing to Explore
A Job Application Letter

Prewriting Notes

Now that Arha is free, he might want to get a job other than farming. Choose one of the jobs your class wrote on the board and write it in the left-hand column below. Then list some details about the job, and about the kind of person you think would be good at the job.

In the right-hand column, list some details about Arha that you've learned from the story, especially those that show he would be good at the job you've chosen.

The Job: _____   About Arha:

What a person does in this job: **Things I know Arha can do:**

_____   _____

_____   _____

_____   _____

_____   _____

The person who is right for this job should be: **What kind of person Arha seems to be:**

_____   _____

_____   _____

_____   _____

_____   _____

Writing to Explore
A Job Application Letter

Writing a Draft

Imagine that you are Arha, writing a letter to apply for the new job you chose for him. Don't forget to explain what kinds of things you are good at, and why this would make you a good person to hire.

Dear Sir or Madam:

My name is Arha, and I am applying for the job of _____

_____

I am the right person for this job because _____

_____

_____

_____

_____

_____

_____

For these reasons, I believe you should hire me for the job.

Sincerely,

Arha

Writing Notebook

This is your chance to look back at what you have written in your Reader's Journal, choose a piece you wrote that you like, and make it the best that it can be. Here's how to revise your draft:

1. Choose a Writing to Explain piece you wrote that you would most like to revise.

2 Mark the page with a paper clip or a sticky note and turn in your Reader's Journal to your teacher. Your teacher will write a question or note on pages 114, 118, or 122 for you to think about.

3. Read and think about your teacher's note. Review the story and your Reader's Journal for more ideas.

4. Plan your revised writing in the prewriting notes section on pages 115, 119, or 123. Then write your revised draft on the page after that.

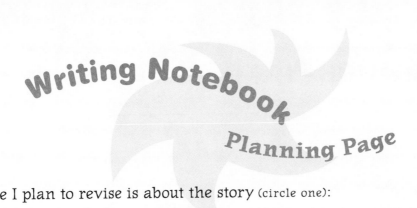

Writing Notebook
Planning Page

The piece I plan to revise is about the story (circle one):

The Banza   **The Man Whose Trade Was Tricks**   **The Fisherman and His Wife**

It is on page _____ of my Reader's Journal.

Think about your teacher's note to help make your writing shine.

_____ **Make your main idea clearer.**

Teacher's note: _____

_____

_____

_____

_____ **Give more evidence to support your main idea.**

Teacher's note: _____

_____

_____

_____

Writing Notebook

Planning Page

Prewriting Notes

Use a web, a chart, or a list to plan your writing.

Writing Notebook

Final Draft

Writing Notebook

Final Draft

Use this page if you need more room.

_____

_____

_____

_____

_____

_____

_____

_____

_____

_____

_____

_____

_____

_____

_____

_____

_____

_____

_____

Writing Notebook
Planning Page

The piece I plan to revise is about the story (circle one):

**Ooka and the
Honest Thief**

**It's All the
Fault of Adam**

**The Monster Who
Grew Small**

It is on page _____ of my Reader's Journal.

Think about your teacher's note to help your writing shine.

_____ **Give more evidence to support your main idea.**

Teacher's note: _____

_____

_____

_____ **Paraphrase story events to use as evidence.**

Teacher's note: _____

_____

_____

_____ **Explain more about how your evidence supports your main idea.**

Teacher's note: _____

_____

_____

Prewriting Notes

Use a web, a chart, or a list to plan your writing.

Writing Notebook
Final Draft

Use this page if you need more room.

_____

_____

_____

_____

_____

_____

_____

_____

_____

_____

_____

_____

_____

_____

_____

_____

_____

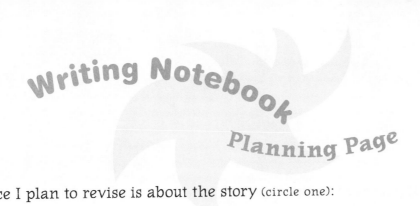

Writing Notebook
Planning Page

The piece I plan to revise is about the story (circle one):

The Selkie Girl   **The Mushroom Man**

The Princess and the Beggar   **The Fire on the Mountain**

It is on page _____ of my Reader's Journal.

Think about your teacher's note to help your writing shine.

_____ **Introduce your main idea more clearly.**

Teacher's note: _____

_____

_____

_____ **Make your opening sentence stronger.**

Teacher's note: _____

_____

_____

_____ **Make sure all the ideas in your essay support your essay's main idea.**

Teacher's note: _____

_____

_____

Prewriting Notes

Use a web, a chart, or a list to plan your writing.

Writing Notebook

Final Draft

Writing Notebook

Final Draft

Use this page if you need more room.

_____

_____

_____

_____

_____

_____

_____

_____

_____

_____

_____

_____

_____

_____

_____

_____

_____

_____

Curious Words

For each story, write down a curious word and the page number where the word appears. Then do one of the following:

- Write why you like your curious word, why it seems curious to you, or why you remember it.

- Pretend that one of the characters in the story uses your curious word and write down something the character says.

- Use your curious word in a message—for example, in a birthday or friendship card, in a poem, or in a funny note to a friend.

- Make up a fun way to use the word yourself.

The Banza

Your curious word _____ **page** _____

_____

_____

_____

Your curious word _____ **page** _____

_____

_____

_____

Your curious word _____ **page** _____

_____

_____

_____

Curious Words

The Man Whose Trade Was Tricks

Your curious word _____ **page** _____

_____

_____

_____

Your curious word _____ **page** _____

_____

_____

_____

Your curious word _____ **page** _____

_____

_____

_____

Curious Words

The Fisherman and His Wife

Your curious word _____ **page** _____

_____

_____

_____

Your curious word _____ **page** _____

_____

_____

_____

Your curious word _____ **page** _____

_____

_____

_____

Curious Words

Ooka and the Honest Thief

Your curious word _____ **page** _____

_____

_____

_____

Your curious word _____ **page** _____

_____

_____

_____

Your curious word _____ **page** _____

_____

_____

_____

Curious Words

It's All the Fault of Adam

Your curious word _____ page _____

_____

_____

_____

Your curious word _____ page _____

_____

_____

_____

Your curious word _____ page _____

_____

_____

_____

Curious Words

The Monster Who Grew Small

Your curious word _____ page _____

_____

_____

_____

Your curious word _____ page _____

_____

_____

_____

Your curious word _____ page _____

_____

_____

_____

Curious Words

The Selkie Girl

Your curious word _____ **page** _____

_____

_____

_____

Your curious word _____ **page** _____

_____

_____

_____

Your curious word _____ **page** _____

_____

_____

_____

Curious Words

The Mushroom Man

Your curious word _____ **page** _____

_____

_____

_____

Your curious word _____ **page** _____

_____

_____

_____

Your curious word _____ **page** _____

_____

_____

_____

Curious Words

The Princess and the Beggar

Your curious word _____ **page** _____

_____

_____

_____

Your curious word _____ **page** _____

_____

_____

_____

Your curious word _____ **page** _____

_____

_____

_____

Curious Words

The Fire on the Mountain

Your curious word _____ **page** _____

_____

_____

_____

Your curious word _____ **page** _____

_____

_____

_____

Your curious word _____ **page** _____

_____

_____

_____

Glossary

In this glossary, you'll find definitions for words that you may not know, but that are in the stories you've read. You'll find the meaning of each word as it is used in the story. The word may have other meanings as well, which you can find in a dictionary if you're interested. If you don't find a word here that you are wondering about, go to your dictionary for help.

absolute: Something is **absolute** when it is complete or total. Your teacher might demand **absolute** silence during a test.

accentuated: To **accentuate** is to call special attention to something. Your mother might **accentuate** how dirty your room is by running her finger through the dust on top of your dresser. The baby deer's long eyelashes **accentuated** its big eyes.

acclaimed: You **acclaim** something when you give it enthusiastic praise and approval. You would **acclaim** your friend who won the spelling bee. The crowd **acclaimed** the championship team.

ambled: To **amble** is to walk at a slow pace because you aren't in a hurry. You might **amble** through a park on the first sunny day of spring. The cows **ambled** to the field to eat grass.

ancient: Very old. People, things, and places that have been around for many, many years can all be described as **ancient**.

angled: To **angle** is to fish with a fishing rod, a hook, and a line, instead of with a net.

antics: Actions that are funny or silly. You would be amused by the **antics** of the clowns at a circus. Your **antics** in class might make your friends laugh, but they could get you in trouble with the teacher.

astonished: You are **astonished** when you are surprised or shocked by something because it is so unusual or unexpected. You might be **astonished** if you saw a kindergartener writing a story or hitting a ball as well as a third grader would.

bale: A large bundle of material tightly tied together. You might see a **bale** of hay on a farm.

banished: To **banish** is to punish someone by making him or her leave or go far away. A coach might **banish** a player from the team for starting a fight during a game. The king **banished** the thief from his kingdom by sending him to a prison thousands of miles away.

barge: A long, large boat with a flat bottom used to carry goods on rivers and canals. A **barge** delivers grain once a month to the towns along the river.

basking: To **bask** is to sit by or lie in a pleasant warmth. People like to **bask** in the sun by the swimming pool. On a cold night of a camping trip, you might spend time **basking** by the fire.

bidding: An order or command. A first grader might do the **bidding** of an older brother or sister.

boisterous: If you are **boisterous** you behave in a noisy and wild way. If your team has won a championship game, you might be **boisterous** at the awards ceremony. Students are allowed to behave **boisterously** sometimes at recess, but not in class.

boon: A favor. It would be a great **boon** if your friend loaned you an umbrella on a rainy day.

bounded: When you **bound**, you move by quick leaps and jumps. The frightened deer **bounded** into the woods for safety. The dog **bounded** out of the house to greet the boy when he came home from school.

brocade: A heavy woven fabric with raised designs on it. The queen wore a robe of gold **brocade**.

case: A special set of facts. A **case** of chicken pox would keep you away from school. If you refused to do what your teacher asked, it would be a **case** of disobedience.

cataract: A very large, steep waterfall.

chanced: If you **chance** to do something, you come across it accidentally or by surprise. You might **chance** to meet your teacher at the shopping center during spring break. If you found a toy car while searching for a ball in the bushes, you could say you **chanced** upon the car.

characters: Letters, figures, or other marks used in printing. All the letters of the alphabet are **characters**. A computer password is usually no more than eight **characters**.

charges: A **charge** is an official statement that accuses someone of doing something wrong or illegal. The police arrested the person on a **charge** of reckless driving. If a jury decides that the person on trial is not guilty, then all **charges** are dismissed.

cherkasska: A long overcoat.

clasped: You **clasp** something when you hold it firmly and tightly. You would want to **clasp** the handrail if the stairs were covered with ice. The woman **clasped** her purse tightly against her chest for fear of losing it.

clenched: When you **clench** something, you squeeze or bring something together. You might **clench** your teeth when you're angry. When you were young, you may have **clenched** your grandfather's hand when he took you somewhere new.

clutched: If something is being **clutched,** it is being held on to tightly. I kept my dog's leash **clutched** in my hand so she wouldn't run away.

commoner: A **commoner** is someone of no special rank or position. In countries with kings and queens, **commoners** are people who are not part of the royal family or system. A prince may be unable to marry a woman he loves because she is a **commoner**.

compound: An area of land with buildings that is usually fenced in.

concealed: To **conceal** is to hide something. The student **concealed** the snack so that the teacher couldn't see it.

conditions: A **condition** is something that is needed before another thing can happen or be allowed. Singing well and attending practice are **conditions** for being in the choir.

conscientious: If you are **conscientious**, that means you know right from wrong and you act according to what you think is right. A **conscientious** student would not cheat on a test. Being **conscientious** also means to take the time and care to do things correctly. You would be **conscientious** if you double-checked your homework for any spelling mistakes.

consoled: To **console** is to comfort or cheer. You try to **console** a person who is sad or disappointed about something. After losing the contest, the boy **consoled** himself by saying he'd try again next year.

contemplation: The act of looking at or thinking about something for a long time. A waterfall or stream is a good place for rest and **contemplation**.

contented: If you are **contented**, you are happy with what you have and are not wishing for anything else. If you feel **contented** after eating a big meal and a special dessert, you wouldn't want to have any more food. A baby can be **contented** with a block or a rattle, while an older child likes to play with more complicated toys.

courage: The quality that makes a person bravely face danger or difficulty. You would show **courage** if you sang in front of a big group of people even though the last time you did it you forgot the words to the song. Firefighters have great **courage** when they go into burning buildings to save people.

court: The king or queen's royal family, personal servants, advisers, and ministers. The king ordered all the people in his **court** to come to the royal ball.

courtesy: Politeness and thoughtfulness, and having good manners. You show **courtesy** when you write thank-you notes for your birthday presents. Your little sister is learning **courtesy** when you teach her how to share toys and take turns.

croft: A small farm, usually with an enclosed field or pasture near the house.

cubits: A **cubit** is a measure of length that is about seventeen to twenty-two inches. Three **cubits** is equal to about five feet. In ancient times, a **cubit** was measured from the elbow to the tip of the middle finger.

declared: You **declare** something when you say it openly and strongly. If you win a spelling bee, the announcer would **declare** you the winner. The team captain **declared** that he was in charge and that his team had to listen to him.

delicacy: A **delicacy** is something pleasing and special, especially a food that is not part of an ordinary meal. If you went to a fancy party, you might describe the raspberry chocolate tart you ate for dessert as a **delicacy**.

demanded: To **demand** is to order something to be done. Your mom might **demand** that you clean up your room, "or else!" When my friend grabbed my favorite pencil out of my hand, I **demanded** that she give it back.

desperate: You are **desperate** when you feel hopeless about something or when you feel you need to do something very badly. You might feel **desperate** if you had only a few minutes left to answer several questions on an important test. A lost pet can become **desperate** for food and water.

destiny: What becomes of a person or thing in the future. If you like animals and science, it might be your **destiny** to be a veterinarian when you grow up. If you never water a plant, its **destiny** is to die sooner than it should.

devour: To eat fast, taking big bites. If you were to play outside for hours, you might get very hungry and **devour** your lunch afterward.

dignity: Your sense of self, pride, or honor is your **dignity**. If you fall down in front of a group of people, you might act as if nothing happened to keep your **dignity**. She won the spelling contest with **dignity**, congratulating the other contestants and being very polite to the judges.

disposition: A person's usual mood or attitude. You might say your friend has a pleasant **disposition** if he is always nice to other people. If you have a crabby **disposition**, others might think of you as rude or hard to talk to.

doomed: Someone or something that is **doomed** will suffer a terrible or unhappy fate. A very nasty person might be **doomed** to live the rest of his life without any friends.

dreadful: Something that is bad or awful. You might think another student's behavior in the classroom is **dreadful** if that student hurts people's feelings or doesn't listen to the teacher. **Dreadful** can also describe something that you are afraid of. You might describe spending a night in a haunted house as **dreadful**.

durra: A kind of grain grown in parts of Africa and Asia.

endure: When you **endure** something, that means you put up with it even if it is unpleasant or painful. You might have to **endure** below-freezing temperatures when walking to school in the winter. If your baby sister can't **endure** your teasing, she might start to cry.

esteemed: If a person is **esteemed**, he or she is someone others respect and have a high opinion of. A teacher whom all students trust and believe is fair might be thought of as an **esteemed** teacher.

exasperation: A feeling of being annoyed and frustrated. You would feel **exasperation** if your friend kept asking you to do something you didn't want to do. Your mom might show her **exasperation** if you and your brother or sister won't stop fighting.

exploits: An **exploit** is a bold and daring act. The superhero's **exploits** saved the day.

exquisite: Something very lovely is **exquisite**. The different shades of pink in the sky at sunset are **exquisite**.

famine: An extreme lack of food. During a **famine**, people starve because they don't have enough to eat.

festive: Merry and joyous. You would be in a **festive** mood at your birthday party. The school might be more **festive** than usual right before summer vacation.

forbidden: If something is **forbidden**, that means it is not allowed. You might be **forbidden** from playing games until you finish your homework. It might be **forbidden** for other people to open your book bag or your locker without your permission.

forlorn: Left alone and sad. You might feel **forlorn** if you were left at home while everyone else in your family went to see a movie, or if you have to wait at the bus stop in the rain all by yourself.

fortnight: Two weeks. If you tell a friend that you will see him in a **fortnight**, that means you will see him in two weeks.

frivolous: If something is not very serious or is of little importance, it is **frivolous**. Watching lots of cartoons might be a **frivolous** thing to do, but it's fun!

fulfill: To **fulfill** means to meet or satisfy. You might not get a part in the play because you can't **fulfill** the requirement to rehearse every day. You also **fulfill** something when you carry out or finish it. If you do get a part in the play, you'd **fulfill** your dream to act onstage.

gazed: To **gaze** is to look at something steadily, especially something beautiful or amazing. You might **gaze** at a rainbow or at a whale swimming. The child **gazed** out the window at the butterflies darting around the bushes.

gleamed, gleaming: Something is **gleaming** if it is shining brightly. Your grandmother might ask you to polish the silverware until it is **gleaming**. The new-fallen snow **gleamed** in the moonlight.

grating: Unpleasant and annoying, usually used to describe a sound. Many people think the noise of fingernails on a chalkboard is **grating**.

gravely: When you are doing or saying something **gravely**, you are doing it in a very serious way. Your parents might speak **gravely** to each other about a family member who has been injured in a car accident. You might look **gravely** at your puppy if it chewed up your shoe.

hearth: The floor of a fireplace and the area in front of it.

herald: Someone who carries messages or makes announcements. In the past, a **herald** might have done so for a king or queen.

honorable: Someone who is honest and shows a sense of what is right and proper is **honorable**. You would be **honorable** if you told the truth even if you knew it might get you into trouble.

indignantly: If you do or say something **indignantly**, you are upset because you feel that something is not fair. You might stomp off to your room **indignantly** if your parents punished you for something you didn't do.

intently: When people do things **intently,** they focus on what they're doing and give it all their attention. Basketball players need to look at the basket **intently** when they try to make a free throw.

interest: An amount of money someone pays for the use of borrowed money. For example, if a bank lends someone money to buy a house, that person will pay the bank back all the money *plus* the **interest** that the bank charges for the loan. And when you put your money in the bank, the bank will pay *you* **interest**, because the bank is borrowing and using your money.

Irù kèrè: A specially prepared white cow's tail that Nigerian kings hold in front of their mouths whenever they speak, since it is considered improper for a king to be seen opening his mouth in public.

keen: Very sharp. A **keen** knife is an important tool to have in the kitchen.

lamentation: Crying and moaning with great sadness. You might hear **lamentation** after something very sad occurs, such as the loss of a loved one.

larder: A small room or closet where food is stored. If your **larder** is empty, you will not be able to make lunch.

lilting: A **lilting** sound is gentle and cheerful. If you sing a **lilting** song, you are singing in a light, happy way.

lineage: Your **lineage** is made up of all the members in your family who came before you, such as your parents, your grandparents, your great-grandparents, and so on. Sometimes you can trace a person's **lineage** back to long ago. An animal's **lineage** helps you figure out whether its family was healthy and strong. That horse came from a long **lineage** of fast runners.

magistrate: A judge. The **magistrate** listened carefully to the accused man before deciding how to punish him.

marrow: The soft material that fills the inside of bones. **Marrow** is used by your body to produce red and white blood cells.

marshaled: When you **marshal** a group of people or things, you gather them together and organize them for a purpose. A general will **marshal** his troops before going into battle. The student **marshaled** all of her ideas and evidence before starting to write her essay.

marveled: You **marvel** at something that fills you with wonder and surprise. He **marveled** at how large and deep the Grand Canyon was when he saw it in person.

merchant: A person who buys and sells things for a living. There is a jewelry **merchant** at the mall who sells pretty necklaces. A **merchant** can also be the owner or manager of a store. All the **merchants** in town decorate their shop windows during the holidays.

middlings: When wheat kernels are ground up at a mill, the smaller, finer bits of flour are removed, and rougher, coarser bits called **middlings** are left over. **Middlings** are used mostly as food for animals.

misfortunes: Your **misfortunes** are the unlucky things that happen to you. You might have the **misfortune** to get sick during the holidays or to pick a rainy day for an outing at the zoo.

mock: To make fun of something or someone in a mean way. Someone who **mocks** you might call you nasty names or imitate you behind your back.

murmured: To **murmur** something is to say it in a soft, quiet voice. You should **murmur** rather than shout when you are in the library. The shy student **murmured** an answer that the teacher could barely hear.

nabbed: If you **nab** something, you seize it or catch it quickly. My sister will always **nab** the last cookie from the jar before I can get it. The police officers **nabbed** the robber escaping out the window.

nourishment: Things that provide **nourishment** are things that you need to live and grow, like food and water. It is important to get **nourishment** from healthy foods.

obliged: You are **obliged** to do something when you have to do it—you have no choice. People are obliged to stop when a police officer holds up his hand. If you broke your neighbor's window playing ball, you would be **obliged** to pay for a new window. You may also be **obliged** to do something because it is important. You might be **obliged** to go back and get your homework assignment if you left it in your desk.

ordeal: An **ordeal** is a difficult or painful experience or test. If you broke your arm falling out of a tree and had to get a cast, you could describe the experience as an **ordeal**. Going through a natural disaster like an earthquake or a tornado would be an **ordeal**.

pages: In the past, a **page** was a boy who worked as a helper for a person such as a king, a queen, or a knight.

paid no heed: When you **pay no heed** to something, you don't give it any careful thought or attention. If you **paid no heed** to fire drill instructions, you might not know how to escape from a burning building. Usually, you **pay heed** to a warning so that you can be on guard or protect yourself.

pavilion: A **pavilion** is a tent or building used for shows, displays, or other kinds of entertainment. It is usually built in a public space. The musicians played in the **pavilion** in the park.

peasants: In earlier times, a person who worked on a farm was called a **peasant**. In the past, there were many **peasants** in Europe and parts of Asia.

persuasion: When you try to talk another person into doing or thinking something by giving good reasons, you are using **persuasion** on that person. If you want to eat dessert before dinner, you might use **persuasion**. You might try **persuasion** to get your sister to clean your room for you.

pestilence: Deadly sickness or disease.

piazza: An open space surrounded by columns and a partial roof.

plague: Something that bothers and annoys you, or causes problems and makes you unhappy. A **plague** of mosquitoes can ruin a nice summer evening.

plaintively: Saying something **plaintively** means you say it in a sad and mournful way. "I miss my mom," the camper said **plaintively** to the camp counselor.

plateau: An area of high, flat land. He could look down on the entire city when he climbed up to the **plateau**.

pleading: To **plead** is to beg or ask for something with all your heart. You might **plead** with your friend to let you borrow a new game. The children kept **pleading** for ice cream until their baby-sitter gave in.

plunged: To **plunge** is to dive into something very fast, without thinking too much about it. Sometimes, when you **plunge** into something, you are doing it fearlessly. You **plunge** into a lake, or you **plunge** into an activity.

precious: Something that is **precious** is very valuable and special, and often it can't be replaced. Diamonds, rubies, and emeralds are called **precious** gems, and parents think of their children as **precious.**

procession: A number of people walking or driving along a path together, usually as part of a celebration. The parade started with a **procession** of people playing musical instruments and having fun.

proclaimed: If you **proclaim** something, you announce it in public. The mayor **proclaimed** the new shopping mall open for business. I **proclaim** that this bicycle is mine and nobody else can ride it!

profusely: When you do something **profusely**, you do it plenty of times—maybe even more than enough. I apologized **profusely** for accidentally hitting my friend with the ball while we were playing catch.

prostrated: To **prostrate** yourself is to lie face down on the ground as a sign of respect or worship. She **prostrated** herself before the throne of the mighty queen.

protested: When you **protest**, you object to or complain about something that bothers or upsets you. You might **protest** against being sent to bed too early. The children **protested** loudly when they were told to turn off the television.

rebuked: To scold someone sharply for something they have done wrong. You could be **rebuked** by your parents for bringing home a poor report card, or you might **rebuke** your sister for borrowing your sweater without asking first.

recklessly: If you do something **recklessly**, you do it without thinking about your own or other people's safety. He **recklessly** ran across the street without checking to see if any cars were coming.

redeem: When you **redeem** something, you are saving it or getting it back when it seems like you are about to lose it. If you were to keep making mistakes in a soccer game, you could **redeem** your standing as a good player by scoring three goals in a row.

reputation: Your **reputation** is the way people think about you. It is what you become known for. You can have a **reputation** for something people value or respect, such as being smart or helpful. You can also have a **reputation** for something people do not like, such as being rude or showing off.

resentment: A feeling of anger about something that has been done or said to you. You might feel **resentment** toward your parents for giving you so many chores to do. You might also feel **resentment** at being made fun of by your older brother.

restless: If you are **restless**, you have a hard time feeling satisfied. You may have a hard time keeping still—you want to be somewhere else or to do something different. Students often get **restless** near the end of the school year. You might get **restless** on a long car trip if you've forgotten to bring any books or games.

restored: Something **restored** has been brought back to its original condition. Your good mood could be **restored** when the sun finally comes out after a long, rainy day.

ridicule: Words or action used to make fun of someone or something. If you make fun of what someone is wearing, your mother might not allow such **ridicule**.

rooted: When you are **rooted** to something or someplace, it means that you cannot or will not move. If your friend wanted to change seats with you at the movies and you didn't want to, you could stay **rooted** to your chair. If a large dog suddenly jumped out at you from behind some bushes, you might be **rooted** to the spot in surprise.

scepter: A long rod that a ruler carries as a sign of power.

scholars: A **scholar** is a person who has lots of knowledge. A group of **scholars** tried to solve the riddle, but it was just too difficult. **Scholar** is also another word used to describe a student. Two of my teachers were history **scholars** when they were in college.

scorched: To **scorch** something is to burn its surface. My father **scorched** his shirt when he set the hot iron down on it. If you stand too close to the fire, it might **scorch** you.

scorn: A strong feeling of dislike for something you think is bad or worthless. You might feel **scorn** for anyone who commits a crime. I felt **scorn** for the boy who made fun of me on the bus, because he teases me only to get attention from the older kids.

scroll: A roll of paper or *parchment* (specially prepared animal skin) with writing on it. Each end of a **scroll** is usually wrapped around a rod.

shamed: To **shame** someone is to cause that person to feel guilty and embarrassed about something they have done. My teacher **shamed** me by sending me to the principal's office in front of the whole class.

simplicity: The quality of being plain and simple. The **simplicity** of the toy made it easy to put together.

snickered: To **snicker** is to laugh in a sneaky, disrespectful way. Someone might **snicker** quietly in class at a silly joke. The children smiled nicely at the woman with the strange haircut, but they **snickered** as soon as she left the room.

spectators: People watching something happen but not participating in it. My older brother was marching in the parade, but my parents and I were only **spectators**. There were many **spectators** at the football game.

spunk: If people say you have **spunk**, they think that you have spirit and bravery. Reading a poem you wrote in front of your whole class would take a lot of **spunk**.

stout: A person who is **stout** has a thick, heavy body. The man had grown too **stout** to fit into his pants.

sufficient: Enough, or as much as someone would need or want. If you weren't very hungry, half a sandwich might be **sufficient** for lunch. If you have as many crayons as you need to make a nice picture, you have a **sufficient** amount.

tantalizing: Something is **tantalizing** if you want it very badly but you cannot have it right away. A piece of chocolate cake is **tantalizing** if you know you have to finish your homework before you can eat it.

tapestry: A heavy piece of cloth with designs or pictures woven into it. A **tapestry** is usually hung on a wall as a decoration and as a way to make the rooms and passageways warmer.

tended, tending: If you **tend** to something, you take care of it. I **tended** to my neighbors' cat while they were on vacation. The farmer is **tending** to the fields, making sure the crops get enough water and sunlight.

thatch: A roof covering made out of strong plant stalks, like straw, reeds, or palm tree leaves.

thrusting: To **thrust** is to push or go through or into something. You may **thrust** yourself through a small opening in a fence to get to the other side. If you're playing soccer with some friends, you could mark where each goalpost would be by **thrusting** a sharp stick into the ground.

till: When you **till** a piece of land, you prepare it for growing crops. A farmer **tills** the soil with a plow to make it easier to plant seeds.

trade: What someone does for a job, especially work that you need special skills to do. My neighbor wants to learn the carpentry **trade** after graduation. My aunt is a musician by **trade**.

trappings: Decorations and ornaments that make something look beautiful. People cover Christmas trees with **trappings** like lights and tinsel. **Trappings** can also make things look expensive. Cinderella went to the ball in a carriage with gold and silver **trappings**.

trembling: If you are **trembling**, that means you are shaking, usually because you are afraid or cold, though it could also be because you are especially excited or angry or weak. During the huge thunderstorm, my new puppy was **trembling** and crying.

unkempt: Something **unkempt** does not look neat and tidy. Your hair would be **unkempt** if you forgot to brush it, or you could have an **unkempt** room if you didn't clean it up.

virtue: If you are a person of **virtue**, it means you know and do what is good. When you are honest, kind, or helpful, you are showing **virtue**.

viziers: A **vizier** is someone who has a very important job in the government and gives advice to the ruler. The word **vizier** was especially used in the Ottoman Empire, which included parts of Asia, Africa, and Europe.